*Key History
for Key Stage 3*

The Twentieth Century World

TEACHER'S GUIDE

*Neil DeMarco and
Richard Radway*

Stanley Thornes (Publishers) Ltd

Applications for such permission should be addressed to the
publishers: Stanley Thornes (Publishers) Ltd, Ellenborough House,
Wellington Street, CHELTENHAM GL50 1YW, England.

First published in 1995 by:
Stanley Thornes (Publishers) Ltd
Ellenborough House
Wellington Street
CHELTENHAM GL50 1YW
England

96 97 98 99 00 / 10 9 8 7 6 5 4 3 2

A catalogue record for this book is available from the British Library.

ISBN 0-7487-2200-9

Contents

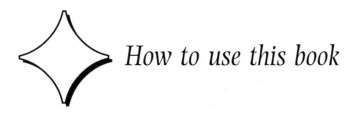

How to use this book

Chapter 2 Europe at war

The first unit of this chapter, 'Great Power rivalry', is intended to give a simple introduction to what is a complicated topic – the long-term causes of the First World War. As with all of the Outline material in the Pupils' Book, this chapter reflects the requirements in the Key Elements for an overview of the main events and developments in the Programme of Study. The questions also concentrate on the Key Element which requires pupils to describe, analyse and explain reasons for, and the results of, historical events.

The questions on page 8, which are based on Source E, should help to reinforce the idea of the Great Powers playing a diplomatic game with one another, trying to score points and gain an advantage over their rivals.

The second unit, 'The outbreak of war', takes this a stage further by looking at the year 1914. In particular it asks students to decide whether Germany was to blame for starting the war. This is an important point, since continental, and not just German historians, tend to criticise British school history books for giving the impression that Germany was largely to blame. By using Unit One alongside Unit Two, showing how all the powers were involved in the diplomatic game, hopefully a more balanced assessment can be made.

This historiographical point is picked up in question 6 on the Causes of the First World War worksheet. This gives pupils an opportunity to decide for themselves who was responsible for the outbreak of the war. This open-ended question allows for a range of responses from the simplistic monocausal to the complex multicausal. It also offers the chance for a piece of extended writing.

The final unit in this chapter, 'Battlefronts on land and sea', gives a brief overview of the course of the war.

Chapter 3 The Western Front (Depth Study)

This Depth Study, with its accompanying Focus Study on art and poetry, provides a closer look at the nature of the fighting and its effects. It relates to the Key Element which requires that pupils should have the opportunity to extend their knowledge by learning about aspects of the Programme of Study in depth. The material also allows access to the Key Element which requires that pupils be taught history from a variety of perspectives. This is achieved by looking at the war's social, cultural and aesthetic aspects. Source A gives an easily accessible overview of the problems of warfare on the Western Front. It might be a useful reinforcement exercise at the end of the unit to ask the students to work out what information about the Western Front they can discover in the chapter which is not shown in Source A.

The unit on new weapons is intended to make clear that at first these did not work as well as expected. Getting students to list the strengths and weaknesses of each weapon could be a useful comprehension exercise.

The unit on The Battle of the Somme enables the student to study the war in depth. Beaumont Hamel is an excellently preserved site, and having now led eight study trips to the battlefields with our students we can strongly recommend a visit. The level of understanding and motivation gained by the students from these visits have to be seen to be believed. Years later students may still recall it as the best experience they gained during their school life. Do note that on Source B the distance between the Hawthorn Crater and the battlefield at Beaumont Hamel has been foreshortened in order to fit the diagram on to the page.

The worksheets on the preparations for a battle should help pupils to understand the problems involved, and it might be useful to get them to compare their decisions with those made on 1 July and then to explain the differences.

As this is a Depth Study, the investigation in the final unit, 'Life in the trenches', includes work based on source analysis. The new level descriptions still require students to be able to evaluate and use sources critically throughout the higher levels.

Focus Study: Art and poetry in the First World War

This is an important unit. It allows students access to different source material to that found elsewhere in the book. It is also important as a cultural element in the Programme of Study.

However, it has to be admitted that First World War poetry was not written with schoolchildren in mind. The language and the allusions are often very difficult for them to cope with. Therefore I have used only sections from the poems, omitting verses which might cause problems of understanding. If you would prefer to use the poems complete, then anthologies are easily obtainable. In our own school the English department has a complete set of *Men who March Away* (published by Heinemann), and there is the *Penguin Book of First World War Poetry* (published by Penguin and edited by Jon Silkin). Sassoon in particular is not an easy poet for students of Key Stage 3. Therefore the worksheet really should be seen as an integral part of the chapter. The intention is to draw out the main historical points from the two poems.

These Sassoon poems are still beyond low-ability pupils, and yet it would be a mistake to deny them access to the poetry of the First World War. Therefore we have included a separate worksheet based on a much simpler Sassoon poem, *The General*. The two worksheets together should stretch the very able, while also enabling lower-ability pupils to benefit from using the material.

Source I comes from that remarkable institution, the *Wiper's Times*. It was first published on 12 February 1916, after Captain F.J. Roberts of the 12th Battalion Sherwood Foresters found a shell-shattered printing house at Ypres. He continued to publish further issues throughout the war. Each time the battalion moved on, so the name of the paper changed. On 3 July 1916 it became the *Kemmel Times* and later that month the *Somme Times*. Roberts became part of that epic battle, during which he was mentioned in dispatches. Towards the end of the war it became known as the *Better Times*. It provides an excellent insight into the experience of a soldier in the First World War, though unsurprisingly the humour is hardly likely to appeal to a Key Stage 3 student. Nonetheless, it is a valuable source and Macmillan have published a complete facsimile of all the issues, in paperback.

Chapter 4 Post-war Europe

This chapter illustrates the Key Elements of the Programme of Study by developing a blend of political, social and economic issues which have their roots in the First World War.

The first unit – 'From the Great War to the 'Great Peace'' – begins by picking up a theme developed at length in Chapter 9: the impact of the First World War on women. This should help to establish in pupils' minds the way in which women emerged from the war with more confidence and with more freedom than before. This chapter also suggests reasons for the changes in social and political attitudes in the years following the Great War.

The map-related questions on page 28 (using the maps in Sources C and D) should help pupils to fix in their minds the countries referred to in Chapter 7 on the Second World War, and at the same time give them an idea of the impact of the Treaty of Versailles.

An opportunity for source evaluation is provided in the unit on 'Changing attitudes and declining prosperity'. It may be worth pointing out that all the written sources in this unit are from privates or NCOs, and this suggests a further line of enquiry for the more able: would the *officers* have expressed similar sentiments? This is a moot point and well-reasoned answers could go either way.

Worksheets to support this chapter are provided for both higher and lower-ability pupils. The first two worksheets are structured writing exercises and text-based questions. This reflects the requirement in the Key Elements for the need 'to develop overviews of the main events and changes'. Both worksheets focus on the impact of the war, with the higher-ability exercise asking pupils to consider that the war helped to speed up the *rate* of political and economic change.

The third worksheet looks at the effects of the First World War on Britain's economy. It deals with statistical evaluation and guides pupils in how to set up and properly label a graph. Question 3 is designed to make pupils aware of the

need for corroborative evidence before confident judgments can be made.

Chapter 5 National Socialist Germany (Depth Study)

This chapter looks at the rise to power of the Nazi Party, and examines its policies once in power. The focus on the impact of Nazi policies on women could serve as a contrast to the Depth Study on women in Britain up to 1945 (Chapter 9). This will help pupils understand how different historical periods relate to one another and the cultural and social diversity within them (Key Element 2a in the revised orders 'Range and depth of historical knowledge and understanding').

There is a further statistical exercise on page 33, to get across the correlation between the effects of the Depression and support for the Nazis. More sophisticated responses might note that the decline in support for the Nazi Party reflected the drop in unemployment in 1933.

A sub-text for the comparison of posters exercise on page 34 is that the appeal of Nazism was not due exclusively to the effects of the Depression. Hitler had significant support among well-to-do Germans such as Albert Speer, and pupils should be aware that Speer came from a wealthy family.

The final questions in this chapter, on page 36, look at the various methods Hitler used to retain mastery of Germany. The point to note is that political repression alone may not have been enough to secure Hitler's position. Indoctrination and prosperity were also potent weapons.

There are seven worksheets related to this chapter. The first three provide statistical exercises for both ability ranges on the Weimar election results and one (for higher ability) on the success of Nazi economic policy. The third presents the factors which need to be considered in evaluating the prosperity of an economy, such as deficits, surpluses, employment and real wages. It reflects the requirements of the Key Element on Historical Enquiry (4b).

Chapter 6 Britain and America between the wars

Chapter 6 presents students with a variety of material to develop skills in using sources. This allows access to the Key Elements which require that pupils have the opportunity to use a range of sources of information, as well as learning about aspects of the Programme of Study in depth. Sources A–F on pages 41 and 42 are all pictorial sources and the questions ask pupils to extract information and draw conclusions from them.

The questions later in the chapter require more sophisticated skills, such as the appreciation of the relative importance and usefulness of cartoons and photographs as historical sources.

It is worth drawing attention to Source H on page 43 to show them that Communism was present in Britain and not just a 'foreign' ideology. Source H could be linked to Sources C and D on page 45 to explain why people might turn to Communism. Orwell's *The Road to Wigan Pier* contains many other useful descriptions of life in 1930s Britain. Orwell was, of course, a socialist, and fought for the Republicans in the Spanish Civil War. It is worth pointing out to students that Orwell was a socialist who had been educated at Eton!

There are three worksheets relating to this chapter. Two worksheets on the Depression give pupils the opportunity to work with statistics. Sophisticated responses to the final question on the high ability Depression worksheet should show an awareness of what 'success' is. Is it the number of people put back in work or the number back in work for each dollar/pound spent? This will require access to the material in the text.

Chapter 7   Global war

The issue of appeasement is something of an easy target for historians operating with hindsight. The questions on page 52 try to place appeasement in its historical context to show that the policy is at least understandable given the legacy of the Great War and Britain's evident military weakness (Source D). Neither was Chamberlain without his supporters, as Source C makes clear. This allows pupils to consider the sort of issues raised in the Key Element 'Interpretations of History' (3a).

The underlying theme of the material in the two units on the war itself (pages 53–56) is the reasons for the Allied victory. The issue stressed here is the overwhelming superiority of the Allied production of raw materials essential to the war effort – especially oil. On this aspect, the second worksheet gives to exercises based on statistics. A timeline exercise ('Heads and Tails') picks up on the chronology Key Element.

Depth Study: The Holocaust

The Holocaust is approached via the gradual escalation of Nazi brutality from the boycott of Jewish shops in 1933 to the gas chambers. A theme worth bearing in mind is that Hitler first de-humanised the Jews by propaganda, and once this had been accepted, the mass-murder followed.

The chapter also deals with the issue of why the Jews made little attempt at resistance, and though the rising of the Warsaw Ghetto is not dealt with here, it could be discussed as an example of Jewish resistance against hopeless odds.

The Key Elements require a study of 'the social, cultural, religious and ethnic diversity of the societies studied' (2a), and a study of the Holocaust will go some way to meeting this. The topic should also serve as a salutary reminder of the roots and consequences of organised racism.

Depth Study: The destroyer of worlds

The reasons for the dropping of the atom bomb in 1945 has long been a source of heated debate. Source E on page 62 gives the 'official' version, and it might be useful to question the reliability of this source. In contrast, Howard Zinn, quoted in Sources E and F, is a highly polemical writer, who seeks to produce a radical response to every question. His intent is to make people question the established view and so he intends to stress aspects that have been ignored in the past. However, in doing so he gives less weight to arguments for the established view, which may well be supported by greater evidence.

Chapter 8   The soldiers' wars: 1914–45 (Depth Study)

This chapter is a Depth Study which aims to point out contrasts and similarities in soldiers' experience of the two world wars. It examines the following four themes: fear; attitudes to the enemy; motivation and treatment of the wounded.

Pupils are asked to consider whether reliable conclusions can be drawn from a limited range of evidence (for example, question 4 on page 67). This may provide the teacher with an opportunity to raise the issue of reliability and, more pertinently, of typicality.

The final unit on 'Medical treatment' allows cross-curricular work, in so far as medical developments played a significant part in the better treatment afforded the wounded in the Second World War.

The worksheet for lower-ability pupils on 'Attitudes towards the enemy' returns to the issue of sufficiency of evidence by asking pupils whether sources in the Pupils' Book offer enough evidence for a decision to be made about Allied attitudes to the enemy.

Chapter 9   The two world wars and the role of women (Depth Study)

The Key Element focus of this chapter is 'Range and depth of historical knowledge and understanding. The emphasis is on the analysis of change and – by implication – of continuity (2b). The content and context for this is provided by an evaluation of a variety of sources related to the position of women from 1914 to 1945.

The material presented here on the experiences of women both at war and on the home front complements that in the previous chapter. It provides a more human dimension to the *experience* of war of both men and women. A point to bear in mind is that though the Great War *did* see some improvement in the status of women – especially during the war itself – some of these gains were inevitably lost in the inter-war period.

The chapter begins by looking at the position of women before 1914 as an essential reference point against which to measure later progress (or lack thereof). What is not so easily proved, but for which a strong case can be made, is that women emerged from both wars more confident of their own abilities. In the case of the Second World War, Sources E and F suggest that this time women were determined not to give up so easily what they had won.

Chapter 10 The post-war world

The first unit in this chapter on the post-war era looks at the Cold War. It builds on a point made in Chapter 1 – that the political history of the twentieth century revolves around the replacement of the European Great Powers by the two Superpowers. The focus is on one particular incident – the Cuban Missile Crisis. There are both high and low-ability worksheets provided to help students understand why this was in many ways the high point of the Cold War, when it really looked as though a nuclear war was imminent. Source H is from Morrison and Commager, in many ways the doyens of American history writing. They give the *established* view, in contrast to Zinn in the Depth Study on the atom bomb in Chapter 7 (Source F).

The purpose of the United Nations unit is to attempt to give a brief but balanced assessment of an organisation which is rarely studied in schools. The unit looks at the political, social and cultural role of the UN and asks students to assess how successful it has been.

The unit on Reconstruction looks at the major players in World War Two who did not become Superpowers, and looks at how they emerged from the war. It will hopefully give students an insight into the world in which they live, in which Germany and Japan are such major economic powers.

Depth Study: The end of Empire

As a change from the usual countries studied for Decolonisation, this study looks at Kenya. However, in the contrast between Sources F and G on page 94, care should be taken when using Meinertzhagen. His is not a liberal viewpoint, however it might appear. Meinertzhagen was also a pioneer settler in British East Africa and he is described by Elspeth Huxley, the historian of the Kenya Pioneers, as a man who 'killed abundantly and killed for pleasure...animals he killed for sport and tribesmen he killed for duty.' He himself said, 'I have no belief in the sanctity of human life or in the dignity of the human race'. Like Johnstone in Source F he very much believes in Pax Britannica to enforce the rule of law in Africa. It is merely that he is very much more perceptive than most White settlers as to where a policy of settling Black lands will lead. As he also noted 'where medicine men are replaced by political agitators there will be a general rising'.

In complete contrast, Dr. Walter Rodney, quoted in Source J on page 95, is a Guyanan and a socialist. He taught at the University College, Tanzania when that country was ruled by the socialist Julius Nyerere. He takes a very polemical, anti-imperialist viewpoint. In the words of the introduction, the purpose of *How Europe Underdeveloped Africa* is to 'make a small contribution towards reinforcing the conclusion that African development is possible only on the basis of a radical break with the international capitalist system'.

Causes of the First World War

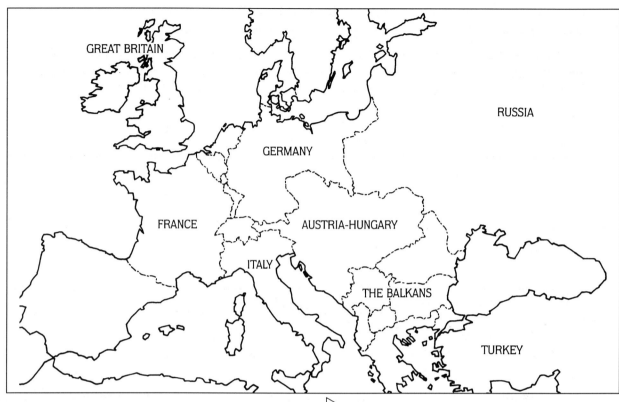

Look at Sources A and B on pages 6 and 7 of your textbook. Then use the outline map above to do the following.

1 Colour in those countries who were members of the Triple Alliance.

2 Use a different colour for those countries who were friends of France.

3 Look at the incomplete sentence below, and decide which of the endings is the right one.

France believed that it would defeat Germany if war broke out because...

> ... the French had helped the Russians to create a modern, powerful army.

> ... the German army was useless.

> ... the Germans were friends of the French and so would never fight them.

4 Here are another three ways of completing a different sentence. Write down which you think is correct.

Germany believed that it would defeat France if war broke out because...

> ... the Germans had a huge airforce.

> ... the Germans would be able to quickly attack and defeat the French before the Russians could attack Germany.

> ... the French were the friends of Britain, who would therefore help the Germans to fight the French

5 Both France and Germany believed that they would win if war broke out. Why does this help to explain why war **did** break out in 1914?

6 Look at pages 9 and 10 of your textbook. They deal with the outbreak of the war and whether or not Germany was to blame.

a) Do you believe that it was Germany's fault that the First World War broke out? Or was it the fault of all the Great Powers?

b) Using the evidence in Chapter 2 of your textbook to back up your argument, explain which of these two statements you agree with.

2B *Preparing for a battle*

Before a battle, the generals had to decide on a plan of action. In the table below there are a list of plans which could be used. Your job is to decide which ones are the best. A plan which might seem good at first might have serious drawbacks.

In the table below, five plans are suggested. For each one there are both **good** points and **bad** points. Your task is to read the good points and bad points and fill in the **Your decision** box with the reason why you are going to use each plan or reject it.

Battle plans	Advantages	Disadvantages	Your decision
1 Cut pathways through your barbed wire so that your troops can get through.	Your troops won't get tangled up in their own barbed wire.	The enemy will be able to line up their machine guns on these pathways.	
2 Order the artillery to fire at the enemy trenches for at least 24 hours.	Many enemy troops may be killed and their barbed wire may be broken.	The enemy will realise an attack is due and so will be ready.	
3 Order the artillery to fire at the enemy trenches for just two hours.	The enemy probably won't realise that an attack is going to happen, and even if they do, they won't have time to bring up reserve troops.	Few enemy troops will be killed.	
4 Bring up troops from the reserve lines to help with the attack.	With more troops your attack is more likely to succeed.	The enemy planes may spot troop movements.	
5 Order artillery to stop firing just before the soldiers attack.	Your own soldiers won't be fired on by your artillery.	The enemy troops will be able to get out of their dug-outs and fire at your troops.	

1 > Which options were used on 1 July?

2 > Which of these helped to produce such heavy casualties?

2c ⟩ *Preparing for a battle*

In the unit called 'A battle in focus' you looked at the Battle of the Somme, which began as a disaster for the British Army but which eventually led to some sort of victory. This exercise helps you to think about the decisions and plans which generals had to make before a battle. Some of the advantages and disadvantages of each battle plan have already been filled in. You must first complete these two columns. Then fill in the final column with your decision – Yes or No – on each option. Would you order this option or not?

Battle plan	Advantages	Disadvantages	Your decision (Yes or No)
1 Dig mass graves to bury the soldiers who are bound to die during the battle.	*If the dead are buried quickly there is less risk of infection*	*The sight of the graves will be bad for the moral of the troops.*	
2 Cut pathways through your barbed wire so that your troops can get through.	*Your troops won't get tangled up in their own barbed wire.*	*The enemy will be able to line up their machine guns on these pathways.*	
3 Order the artillery to fire at the enemy trenches for at least 24 hours.		*The enemy will realise an attack is due and so will be ready.*	
4 Order the artillery to fire at the enemy trenches for just two hours.	*The enemy probably won't realise that an attack is going to happen, and even if they do, they won't have time to bring up reserve troops.*		
5 Bring up troops from the reserve lines to help with the attack.	*With more troops your attack is more likely to succeed.*	*The enemy planes may spot troop movements.*	
6 Order artillery to stop firing just before the soldiers attack.			
7 Order the attack for dawn.			
8 Order troops to take all of their equipment with them.	*They will be able to dig in and hold any stretches of enemy trench which they capture.*		

2c Preparing for a battle

In the unit called 'A battle in focus' you looked at the Battle of the Somme, which began as a disaster for the British Army but which eventually led to some sort of victory. This exercise helps you to think about the decisions and plans which generals had to make before a battle. Some of the advantages and disadvantages of each battle plan have already been filled in. You must first complete these two columns. Then fill in the final column with your decision – Yes or No – on each option. Would you order this option or not?

Battle plan	Advantages	Disadvantages	Your decision (Yes or No)
1 Dig mass graves to bury the soldiers who are bound to die during the battle.	If the dead are buried quickly there is less risk of infection	The sight of the graves will be bad for the morale of the troops.	
2 Cut pathways through your barbed wire so that your troops can get through.	Your troops won't get tangled up in their own barbed wire.	The enemy will be able to line up their machine guns on these pathways.	
3 Order the artillery to fire at the enemy trenches for at least 24 hours.		The enemy will realise an attack is due and so will be ready.	
4 Order the artillery to fire at the enemy trenches for just two hours.	The enemy probably won't realise that an attack is going to happen, and even if they do, they won't have time to bring up reserve troops.		
5 Bring up troops from the reserve lines to help with the attack.	With more troops your attack is more likely to succeed.	The enemy planes may spot troop movements.	
6 Order artillery to stop firing just before the soldiers attack.			
7 Order the attack for dawn.			
8 Order troops to take all of their equipment with them.	They will be able to dig in and hold any stretches of enemy trench which they capture.		

Why was the war 1914–18 known as the 'Great War'?

Until the outbreak of the Second World War in 1939, the 1914–18 war was known as the 'Great War'. Why was this?

A The Global extent of the First World War

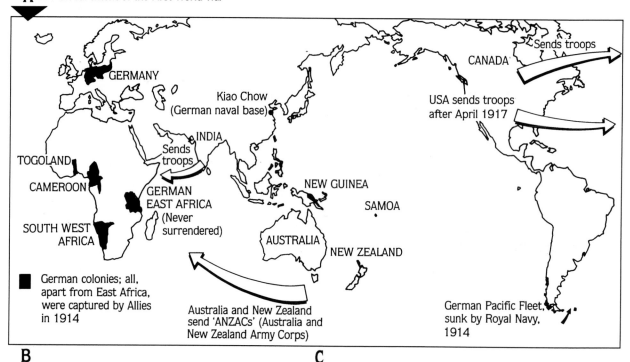

CANADA — Sends troops

USA sends troops after April 1917

GERMANY

Kiao Chow (German naval base)

INDIA Sends troops

TOGOLAND

CAMEROON

GERMAN EAST AFRICA (Never surrendered)

NEW GUINEA

SAMOA

SOUTH WEST AFRICA

AUSTRALIA

NEW ZEALAND

■ German colonies; all, apart from East Africa, were captured by Allies in 1914

Australia and New Zealand send 'ANZACs' (Australia and New Zealand Army Corps)

German Pacific Fleet, sunk by Royal Navy, 1914

B

War deaths per day	
The war between France and Germany 1870–1	approx. 1000
First World War	approx. 5500

C

Military loss of life in the First World War	
France	1.4 million
Britain and the Empire	1 million
Russia	1.7 million
Germany	1.8 million
Austria Hungary	1.2 million

D

British losses on the first day of Battle of the Somme	
Killed	19,240
Missing	2,154
Wounded	35,493

F

E very square mile of trench contained 1 million cubic feet of timber and 900 miles of barbed wire.

(From Aylett, Britain and the Great War, Hodder and Stoughton, 1930)

E General von Motke describing the Battle of Tannenberg

T he sight of thousands of Russians driven into two huge lakes or swamps to drown was ghastly. So fearful was the sight of these thousands of men, with their guns, horses and ammunition, struggling in the water, that to shorten their agony, they [the German soldiers] turned the machine guns on them. But even in spite of that there was movement seen among them for a week or more.

▷ Do you think that the 'Great War' is an accurate description of the First World War? Explain your answer using evidence from Sources A–F.

Western Front Crossword

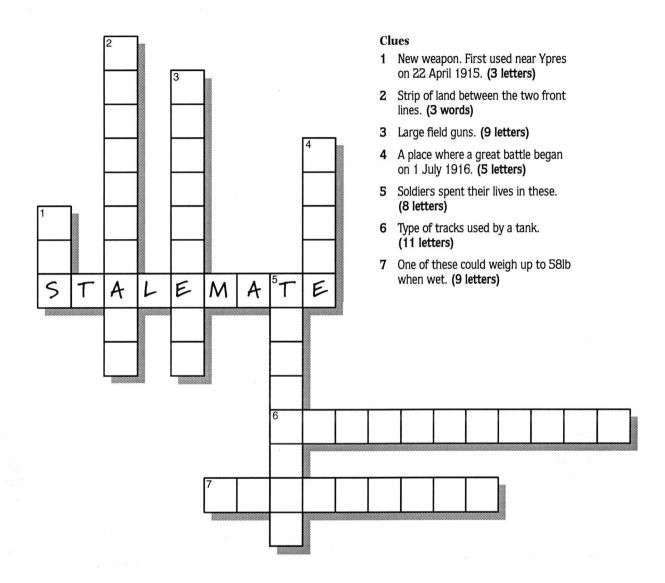

Clues

1 New weapon. First used near Ypres on 22 April 1915. **(3 letters)**

2 Strip of land between the two front lines. **(3 words)**

3 Large field guns. **(9 letters)**

4 A place where a great battle began on 1 July 1916. **(5 letters)**

5 Soldiers spent their lives in these. **(8 letters)**

6 Type of tracks used by a tank. **(11 letters)**

7 One of these could weigh up to 58lb when wet. **(9 letters)**

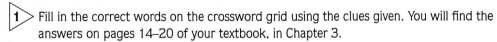

1▷ Fill in the correct words on the crossword grid using the clues given. You will find the answers on pages 14–20 of your textbook, in Chapter 3.

2▷ The answers to Clues 1, 3 and 6 refer to weapons used in the First World War.

a) Which two of these weapons were first used in this war?

b) When these two weapons were first used they were expected to bring the war to a swift end. Explain why both of these weapons failed to work as well as had been expected.

3B *Siegfried Sassoon*

Use this worksheet along with Sources G and H on page 25 of your textbook. These are both poems by Siegfried Sassoon

---

Absolution

…war is our scourge; yet war has made us wise,
And fighting for our freedom, we are free.'

'Horror of wounds and anger at the foe,
And loss of things desired, all these must pass.
We are the happy legion…'

1▷ What do you think the word 'scourge' means?

2▷ 'Fighting for our freedom, we are free.' Why might British soldiers have believed that they were fighting for freedom?

3▷ Are these lines optimistic? Give reasons for your answer.

4▷ Why does Siegfried Sassoon feel that he and his comrades should be happy?

Base Details

'… And speed glum heros to death.'

1▷ Who are the 'glum heroes'?

2▷ Who does Sassoon believe sends them to their death?

3▷ What are these people doing while the heroes die?

4▷ 'I used to know his father well.' What does this suggest about the age of the people at the base?

5▷ Is this poem optimistic? Can you think of another word to describe it? Give reasons for your answer.

6▷ Compare Siegfried Sassoon's views of the war in these two poems. In what ways are they the same? In what ways are they different?

Siegfried Sassoon

Read this poem by Siegfried Sassoon and answer the questions that follow.

The General

'Good-morning; good-morning!' the General said
When we met him last week on our way to the line.
Now the soldiers he smiled at are most of 'em dead,
And we're cursing his staff for incompetent swine.
'He's a cheery old card,' grunted Harry to Jack
As they slogged up to Arras with rifle and pack.

But he did for them both with his plan of attack.

---

1 In line 2 the poet says 'We met him last week on our way to the line'.
What is 'the line'?

2 What does the word 'incompetent' mean?

3 Who does the poet call 'incompetent swine'?

4 **a)** What happens to the two men, Harry and Jack?

  b) Who does the poet blame for this?

5 Does the poet believe that war is good?
Explain your answer.

4A Understanding the Text

These questions are about the effects of the First World War in Europe. You will find the answers in Chapter 4 in your textbook – Post-war Europe – on the page given at the end of the question.

1 What drastic steps was Britain forced to take to win the war? (page 27)

2 **Three** jobs done by women during the war are mentioned on page 27. Which of these do you think would have been the hardest for women to do? Give a reason for your answer.

3 Which **three** European countries faced revolution and street violence after the war? (page 27)

4 Which **four** countries were on the winning side in the First World War? (page 28)

5 What was the name of the treaty signed after the war by Germany and the Allies? (page 28)

6 What did this treaty force Germany to do with her army, navy and air force? (page 28)

7 Which country became the world's first Communist country in 1917? (page 29)

8 How many Russians were killed in the First World War? (page 29)

9 Why did many soldiers after the war feel they had fought for nothing? (page 31)

10 When did the Great Depression begin? (page 32)

Summary activity

Use the following two paragraphs as a summary of what you have read in Chapter 4. Complete the unfinished sentences and add the title 'The effects of the First World War in Europe'.

If you get stuck you can choose the missing words from the list at the bottom of the page, but try using Chapter 4 in your textbook first.

'The First World War gave women the chance to do exciting new jobs such as

_____. The war also changed the map of Europe by creating new

countries. Germany and Austria were on the losing side and had to agree to harsh peace

treaties. Austria's treaty was called _____. Russia had a

revolution during the war and became a Communist country. In 1923 it changed its

name to _____. Italy also had a revolution after the war, but it

became a _____ country under the leadership of the dictator

_____.

One of the reasons for these revolutions is that many _____

returned from the war and found there were no _____ for them.

Many became so angry that they were willing to overthrow the existing

_____.'

Choose from: jobs   The Treaty of St Germain   ambulance drivers   government
                The Union of Soviet Socialist Republics   Mussolini   Fascist   soldiers.

4B *Understanding the Text*

Answer the following questions about Chapter 4 in your textbook – Post-war Europe. After each question is the number of the page where you can find the answer.

1▷ Which of the two images of women shown in Sources A and B on page 27 do you think women's rights campaigners at the time would have approved of? Give reasons for your answer. (page 78)

2▷ Why did Britain not experience revolution after the war as Germany, Russia and Italy did? (page 27)

3▷ After the Treaty of St Germain, the new country of Yugoslavia was created. It consisted of Serbs, Croats and Bosnians. What recent events suggest that these groups had serious differences between them?

4▷ What was unusual about the fact that Italy – as well as Germany – faced revolution after the war? (page 30)

5▷ Why might a harsh treaty against the Germans slow the economic recovery of the Allied powers? (page 29)

6▷ Why was Fascism in Italy unlikely to appeal to workers and peasants? (page 30)

7▷ What evidence is there in the text that revolution appeals to desperate people? (pages 29–32)

8▷ Do you think it's likely that many **officers** would have shared the views of the ordinary soldiers quoted in Sources A–C on page 31? Explain your answer.

9▷ Why was Britain's economy so badly affected by the war? (page 32)

▷ **Extended writing exercise**

Read the following question carefully.

Trotsky, the Russian Communist leader, said 'War is the locomotive of history'. Does the evidence in this chapter support this theory?

Below are some suggestions about how you might think about answering this. You can follow them if you wish, or use your own ideas. You should try to write about 250 words.

First

Explain what Trotsky meant by this phrase. Then look at how the war affected these three important areas: politics; society; the economy.

Politics   How did the map of Europe change after the war?

Could new political ideas like Communism and Fascism have been helped by the war?

Society   Did the war change the attitudes of ordinary men to authority? Were they more or less likely to revolt as a result of the war?

Did attitudes to the role of women change because of the war?

Economy   Were the economies of European countries prosperous after the war? Would problems like unemployment make change more or less likely?

Conclusions

Was Trotsky right? Or would the changes which took place in the 1920s and 1930s have happened anyway even without the war?

The effect of the First World War on Britain's economy

For this worksheet, use the statistics in Source F on page 32 of your textbook.

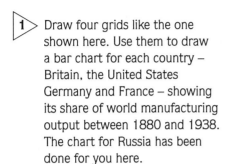

1 ▷ Draw four grids like the one shown here. Use them to draw a bar chart for each country – Britain, the United States Germany and France – showing its share of world manufacturing output between 1880 and 1938. The chart for Russia has been done for you here.

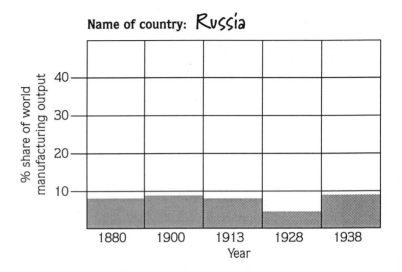

Name of country: Russia

(chart: y-axis labelled "% share of world manufacturing output" with values 10, 20, 30, 40; x-axis labelled "Year" with values 1880, 1900, 1913, 1928, 1938)

2 ▷ The following paragraph tells you what the bar charts show. Only one of the choices in each bracket is true. Copy the paragraph into your exercise book, putting in the choices you think are true.

'In 1880 (Britain/the United States) was the richest country in the world. Between 1880 and 1938 Britain's share of goods (increased/fell). However, (Germany/France) was catching up and by (1900/1913) had actually overtaken Britain as a producer of goods made by machine. In (1928/1938) (the United States/Britain) produced a bigger share of these goods than in 1913.

3 ▷ The bar chart you have just drawn for Britain suggests that the British economy was in trouble during the 1920s. However, one set of statistics is not enough for an historian to make a proper judgement. If the British economy was weak in the 1920's, how would this have affected each of the following? Would the numbers have gone up or down?

a) The number of people out of work in Britain.

b) The quantity of goods sold by Britain to other countries.

c) The number of British companies going out of business.

Give a reason for your answer.

5A Election results in Weimar Germany

German political parties in the period 1919–33 can be divided into two groups:

✦ Those who supported Germany's new **democratic** system ('the Weimar Republic');
✦ Those who wanted to overthrow it.

The People's Party, the Democrats, the Catholic Centre Party, and the Socialists were all supporters of the democratic republic. They are known as the parties of the Weimar Coalition.

The Nazis and the Nationalists were two parties of the *extreme right* who were against democracy. The Communists on the *extreme left* also wanted to overthrow the Weimar republic.

The chart on the second sheet shows the percentage of the vote which the major political parties in Germany achieved in elections during the period of the Weimar Republic.

1 Colour the boxes against each party, using one colour for the parties of the **Weimar Coalition** and another colour to show the **opponents** of the republic.

2 **a)** What percentage of the vote did the parties of the Weimar Coalition get in 1919?
b) What percentage did they get in 1933?

3 **a)** What percentage of the vote did the opponents of the Weimar republic get in 1919?
b) What percentage did they get in 1933?

4 Here are 6 statements about the German election results during this period. Using the chart, say whether each of these statements is **true** or **false**. If a statement is false, write down what the correct version of the statement should be.

For example, the answer to Statement A is **False**: the party whose support grew the most was the Nazis. Their vote increased by more than six times from 1924 to 1933. Write your answers in the table on the second sheet.

A The Communist vote increased the most up to 1933. The number of votes increased by six times from 1920 to 1933.

B The People's Party lost the most support between 1919 and 1933.

C The Catholic Centre Party's vote didn't change very much.

D The Nazi vote increased the most, compared to the other parties, from one election to the next. It went up from 3 per cent to 18 per cent between 1928 and 1930 – a six times increase.

E The People's Party lost the most support from one election to the next, compared with the other parties.

F The People's Party and the Democrats did not get very much support.

5 Can you suggest any reasons why those parties opposed to the republic did so well from 1930 onwards? (Clue: think about the economy).

5A *(continued)*

	1919	1920	1924	1924	1928	1930	1932	1932	1933
☒ Nazi Party	–	–	7	3	3	18	37	33	44
☒ Nationalists	10	15	20	21	14	7	6	8	8
☒ Peoples's Party	4	14	9	10	9	5	1	2	1
☒ Democrats	19	8	6	6	5	4	1	1	1
☒ Catholic Centre Party	20	18	16	18	15	15	16	15	11
☒ Socialists	38	22	21	26	30	25	22	20	18
☒ Communists	–	2	13	9	11	13	14	17	12
☒ Others	9	21	8	7	13	13	3	4	5
	100	100	100	100	100	100	100	100	100

(A dash means that the party was not involved in elections that year.)

Write your answers to question 4 in the table below.

Statement	True or False	Correct statement
A	False	The Nazi vote increased the most up to 1933. It was six times greater in 1933 than in 1924.
B		
C		
D		
E		
F		

Election results in Germany from 1919 to 1933

Between 1919 and 1933 there were two main groups of political parties in Germany:

✦ One group supported Germany's new democratic government;

✦ The other group wanted to use violence to get rid of it.

The parties which **supported** democracy were:

the Socialists,   the Catholic Centre Party,

the Democrats,   the People's Party.

The parties **against** democracy were:

the Nationalists,   the Nazis

the Communists.

The chart on the second page shows the percentage of the vote for each of these parties in the Germany elections between 1919 and 1933. The higher the percentage, the more votes. So, in 1919 the Socialists got the most votes with 38 per cent of the total votes.

1 ▷ Colour the boxes against each party, like this:

  a) Use one colour for those parties which supported the democratic system of government.

  b) Use a different colour for the three parties who wanted to get rid of Germany's democratic government.

2 ▷ Here are 5 sentences about these election results with names of parties or dates missing. Fill in the missing name or date for each sentence. Choose from the list below the sentences.

For example, the answer to **A** is **Socialist Party**.

A   The _____ _____ got the most votes in the 1919 election.

B   The _____ _____ got the least votes in the 1919 election.

C   The party which got the most votes in any election was the _____ _____

D   The Communists got their highest vote in the _____ election.

E   The Socialists got their lowest vote in the _____ election.

  1933   **Socialist Party**   **Nazi Party**

    1932   **People's Party**

3 ▷ **a)** Add up the percentages in the 1919 election of all the parties which **supported** democracy. Do this by adding the 4 per cent of the People's Party to the 19 per cent of the Democrats and

then add the 20 per cent of the Catholic Centre Party and the 30 per cent of the Socialists to make one total.

  b) Now do the same for the three parties who were **against** Germany's democratic government.

  c) Which group had the biggest percentage of the votes?

4 ▷ **a)** Add up the percentages for the parties which **supported democracy** in the 1933 election.

  b) Add up the percentages for the parties which were **against democracy** in the 1933 election.

  c) Which group had the biggest percentage of the votes?

5 ▷ Choose which one of these two sentences you think is true, and complete it using the information from your answers to Questions 3 and 4.

'Between 1919 and 1933 the parties which supported democracy in Germany became more popular because...'

_____

_____

_____

or 'Between 1919 and 1933 the parties which supported democracy became less popular because...'

_____

_____

_____

(continued)

		1919	1920	1924	1924	1928	1930	1932	1932	1933
✖	**Nazi Party**	–	–	7	3	3	18	37	33	44
✖	**Nationalists**	10	15	20	21	14	7	6	8	8
✖	**Peoples's Party**	4	14	9	10	9	5	1	2	1
✖	**Democrats**	19	8	6	6	5	4	1	1	1
✖	**Catholic Centre Party**	20	18	16	18	15	15	16	15	11
✖	**Socialists**	38	22	21	26	30	25	22	20	18
✖	**Communists**	–	2	13	9	11	13	14	17	12
✖	**Others**	9	21	8	7	13	13	3	4	5
		100	100	100	100	100	100	100	100	100

NB '–' symbol means that the party was not involved in elections that year.)

5c ◇ *How successful was Nazi economic policy?*

The success of a country's economic policy can be measured in different ways.

For example:

✦ If the value of the goods a country exports (sells to other countries) is more than the value which it imports (buys in from other countries), then it has a **balance of trade surplus**. A balance of trade surplus is considered a good thing. On the other hand, if a country imports more than it exports, then it has a **balance of trade deficit**. This is usually seen as bad news.

✦ **Low unemployment** is another sign of a strong economy. It is also important for wages to increase at the same rate (or more) than prices. For example, if wages increase by 10 per cent in a year while prices only increase by 5 per cent, then workers have seen their **real wages** rise by 5 per cent and so their standard of living has gone up because they can buy more with their wages. Real wages are a measure of what wages can buy.

Study these graphs carefully. They describe what was happening in the German economy before and after Hitler came to power in 1933.

A Value of goods exported and imported in billions of marks

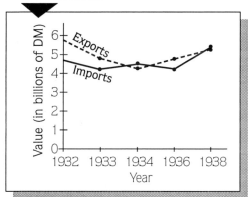

C Real Weekly Wages. These are based on a relative value of 100 for 1932. So, for example, in 1935 wages went up by 10 per cent more than prices. So workers were better off in that year.

1932	1933	1934	1935	1936	1937	1938	1939
100	104	109	110	112	115	119	123

B Number of unemployed (in millions)

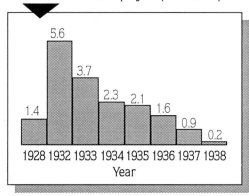

D Size of the German Army (number of infantry battalions)

1933	1934	1935	1936	1937	1938
84	166	287	334	352	476

(Note: By 1939 the German Army had 730,000 men.)

1 ▷ In which years did the German economy show a balance of trade **deficit**?

2 ▷ What happened to the level of unemployment in Germany after Hitler came to power?

3 ▷ What evidence is there in A–C that the standard of living of German people rose between 1933 and 1938?

4 ▷ Opponents of Hitler could claim that his policies were harmful to the economy, and that not all the new jobs created involved making useful products. What evidence is there in these sources to support this claim? (Remember that men in the army were no longer unemployed.)

German war tactics: Blitzkrieg

German army tactics played an important part in Germany's success in the early years of the war against Poland, France and Russia. These tactics, called *Blitzkrieg* or 'lightning war', involved 3 stages.

Stage 1

Enemy headquarters and communications (telephones, radio stations) would be bombed while paratroopers were dropped behind enemy lines. They would cut telephone wires and seize control of bridges and airfields before the enemy could destroy them.

Stage 2

The main attack would take place at great speed with tanks and infantry in trucks (motorised infantry). This spear-head would attack the enemy's weakest points and race towards key targets behind the front line. The best defended sectors would be left to the third stage.

Stage 3

The enemy's strongpoints would be surrounded by troops and cut off from reinforcements. Eventually, they would be forced to surrender after running out of supplies.

The chart on the second sheet shows the 3 stages of a 'Blitzkrieg' attack. In each of the four blank boxes write a brief description of what these forces had to do. For example, in the box labelled 'Foot soldiers' you could write that their job was to follow up behind the main attack, surround the enemy strongpoints and force them to surrender by cutting off supplies.

5D and E (continued)

Airfield

Paratroopers:

Bridge

Town

Divebombers

Divebombers:

Strongpoint

ENEMY FRONTLINE

Strongpoint

Tanks
(motorised infantry)

Tanks
(motorised infantry)

Tanks:

Foot soldiers:

5E   *German war tactics: Blitzkrieg*

German army tactics played an important part in Germany's success in the early years of the war against Poland, France and Russia. These tactics, called *Blitzkrieg* or 'lightning war', involved 3 stages.

Stage 1

Enemy headquarters and communications (telephones, radio stations) would be bombed while paratroopers were dropped from planes behind enemy lines. They would cut telephone wires and seize control of bridges and airfields before the enemy could destroy them.

Stage 2

The main attack would take place at great speed with tanks and infantry in trucks (motorised infantry). This spear-head would attack the enemy's weakest points and race towards key targets behind the front line. The best defended sectors would be left to the third stage.

Stage 3

The enemy's strongpoints would be surrounded by troops and cut off from reinforcements. Eventually, they would be forced to surrender after running out of supplies.

The chart on the second sheet shows the 3 stages of a 'Blitzkrieg' attack. In each of the four blank boxes write a brief description of what these forces had to do. For example, in the box labelled 'Foot soldiers' you could write that their job was to follow up behind the main attack, surround the enemy strongpoints and force them to surrender by cutting off supplies.

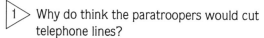
1 Why do think the paratroopers would cut telephone lines?

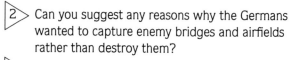
2 Can you suggest any reasons why the Germans wanted to capture enemy bridges and airfields rather than destroy them?

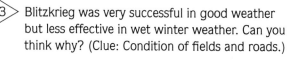
3 Blitzkrieg was very successful in good weather but less effective in wet winter weather. Can you think why? (Clue: Condition of fields and roads.)

5F *Who benefited from Nazi rule?*

This worksheet is based on Chapter 5 of your textbook and the Depth Study on the Holocaust in Chapter 7. That's where you'll find the evidence to complete this exercise. In the chart below are listed 7 groups of people in Germany while Hitler was in power.

For each group you have to:
◆ make a judgement about whether Hitler's policies benefited them or not;
◆ in the next column, give evidence from the text to support your judgement.

You may find some additional evidence on worksheet C for Chapter 5.

	Judgement: Benefited from Nazi rule: Yes or No	Evidence
Wealthy business people		
Workers		
Women		
School girls		
Jews		
Unemployed workers		

5G   *Understanding the text*

Chapter 5 is about how Hitler came to be Chancellor of Germany and how he used his power. The answers to the following questions are in Chapter 5. The page number where you'll find the answer is given at the end of each question.

1 ▷ What was the name of Hitler's party? (page 33)

2 ▷ Who appointed Hitler Chancellor of Germany in January 1933? (page 33)

3 ▷ How many people were unemployed in Germany in the year Hitler was made Chancellor? (look at Source A on page 3)

4 ▷ What were many wealthy Germans afraid of? (page 34)

5 ▷ What groups of people did Hitler detest, apart from democrats? (page 35)

6 ▷ What percentage of the vote did the Nazis get in the elections of March 1933? (page 33)

7 ▷ What were school Biology lessons in Hitler's Germany used to show? (page 37)

8 ▷ At what age could girls join the Young Maidens? (page 37)

9 ▷ Why were women discouraged by the Nazis from smoking and slimming? (page 39)

10 ▷ Who did Hitler kill in 'the Night of the Long Knives'? (read Source A on page 38)

Summary activity

Use the following two paragraphs as a summary of what you have read in Chapter 5. Complete the sentences and give your paragraphs the title 'Hitler's rule in Germany'.

If you get stuck, choose the missing word from the list at the bottom of the page, but try using Chapter 5 on its own first.

'Germany's economic problems between 1929 and _____ were so bad that many Germans were willing to vote for Hitler. He promised the unemployed that he would find _____ for them. He told the rich that he would crush the threat to their wealth from the _____. In 1933 the President, Hindenburg, appointed Hitler as _____. Six months later Hitler had got rid of all other political parties and closed down their newspapers. He was now _____ of Germany.

He used the secret police, known as the _____, against any enemies. He encouraged young German boys and girls to join his Nazi youth movements. Workers were not allowed to go on _____ and their trade unions were banned. He found millions of jobs for the _____. By 1939 Germany was a powerful and _____ country.'

Choose from: **Gestapo   prosperous   1933   Communists   jobs**
                dictator   strike   Chancellor   unemployed

6A *The New Deal*

The American Constitution is a set of rules which say how America is to be governed. In particular it says what the President can and cannot do.

President Roosevelt's New Deal gave many people a better life and more hope for the future. However, the Constitution did not allow Roosevelt to introduce measures which dealt with the pay and working conditions of the people. Many Americans thought that if you allowed the President to break the Constitution there was nothing to stop him becoming a **dictator.**

A The New Deal is shown in this cartoon as the Wooden Horse of Troy

Weidenfeld & Nicholson Archives

1 > What is a **dictator**?

2 > In the cartoon, which group of people are shown as the **defenders** of the American Constitution?

3 > What do you think that the cartoonist means by showing the New Deal as the Trojan Horse?

4 > Does the cartoonist support the New Deal? Explain your answer.

5 > 'Because the cartoon shows only one man's opinion it is of no use to the historian.' Do you agree with this statement? Explain your answer.

The Depression

Unemployment in Britain and the USA

A Unemployment in the USA 1929–38

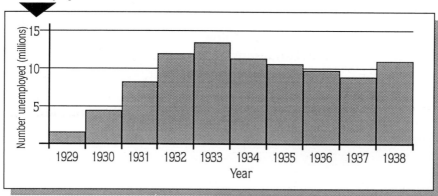

B Unemployment in Britain 1928–38 (millions)

1929	1930	1931	1932	1933	1934	1935	1936	1937	1938
1.4	2.1	2.75	2.8	2.9	2.45	2.4	2.2	1.75	1.9

C Bar chart of unemployment in Britain 1929–38

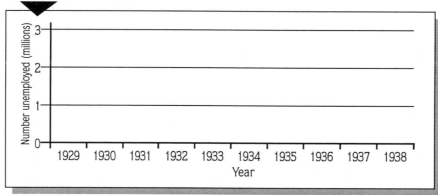

1▷ Using the axes in **C**, draw a bar chart like **A** using the figures for British unemployment given in **B**.

2▷ Which country had more people unemployed in 1932?

3▷ Which country had more people unemployed in 1938?

4▷ Which country was the more successful in getting people back to work? Give the reason for your answer.

6c The Depression

Unemployment in Britain and the USA

A Bar chart of unemployment in Britain 1929–38

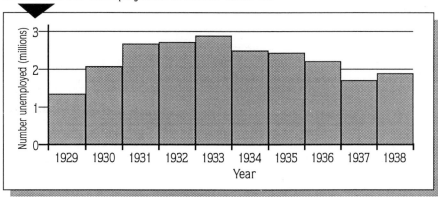

B Unemployment in the USA 1929–38

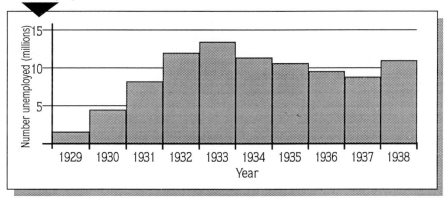

C Population of Britain and America in 1930

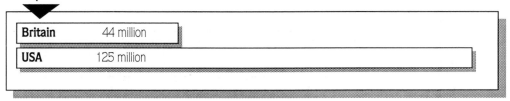

Britain	44 million
USA	125 million

1 Which country had the greater number of people unemployed in 1933?

2 In 1930 which country had the greater proportion of its population unemployed?

3 In 1932 which country had the greater proportion of its population unemployed? Why might this figure be less accurate than your answer to Question 2?

4 According to George Orwell (read Source E on page 45 of your textbook), why might the unemployment figures in **A** and **B** be considered too low?

6c *(continued)*

D British Government spending 1930–38

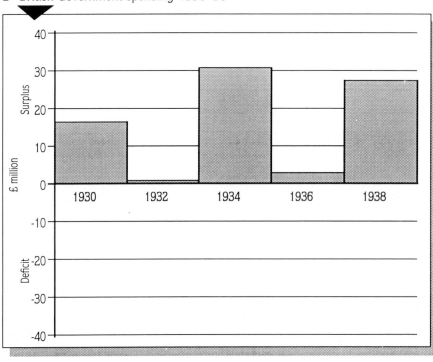

E US Government spending 1930–38

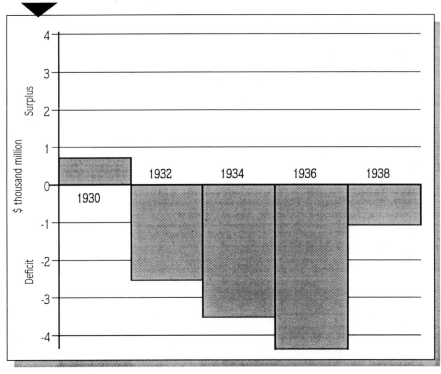

5 > What is meant by the term 'deficit' in **D** and **E**? (see page 47 of your textbook)

6 > **a)** Which government maintained a deficit during the 1930s?

b) Why did they do this?

7 > Which government was more successful in reducing unemployment? Give reasons for your answer.

8 > Look at **D**. Why do you think this allowed the British government to claim that they were more efficient than the US in reducing unemployment?

7A ◇ *Air-raid precautions*

People were encouraged by the government to make their houses as safe as possible against the effects of bombing and gas attacks. Many precautions were taken against bombs:

✦ Windows were taped on the inside to stop the glass being shattered by the blast from a bomb.

✦ Fireplaces and ventilation bricks were sealed up to stop poison gas getting inside the house. (Fortunately, neither side used poison gas during the war.)

✦ A bucket of water and a hand-operated pump were always ready to put out fires caused by incendiary (fire) bombs.

✦ Special shelters, called Anderson Shelters, were built in the garden to provide protection against collapsing buildings. Extra food could be grown on the roof of the shelter and in the rest of the garden. This meant that Britain had to buy less food from other countries.

✦ Iron railings were taken up to be used for making weapons.

✦ Headlamps – even on bicycles – were mostly taped over to make sure that no light could be seen by enemy bombers. (This was because of the blackout, as lights would make it easy for bombers to find their targets.)

Look at the picture on the second sheet. In the labelled boxes explain briefly how each of these precautions might help during an air-raid. Base your answers on the information given on this sheet.

7A (continued)

Sealed fireplace:

Bucket of water and hand pump:

Windows covered with tape:

Masked bicycle headlamp:

Anderson shelter:

Sealed ventilation brick:

Vegetables growing on shelter roof:

Railings removed from wall:

7B *Raw materials and war production*

Supplies of raw materials such as coal, iron ore, oil, and wheat are vital for a country at war. The country or side with the best supply of these raw materials is more likely to win.

A shows the supplies of raw materials that were available to each side – the Allies and the Axis Powers – during the Second World War. **B** shows what the raw materials were used for. Study them both and then answer the questions that follow.

A Supplies of raw materials for the major countries at war

		Coal	Oil	Iron	Copper	Bauxite	Potash	Wheat	TOTAL
Allies	USA	export	export	ss	ex	nss	def	ss	
	USSR	ss	ex	ss	nss	ss	def	ex	
	Britain	ex	def	nss	def	def	def	def	
								Allies total ➡	
Axis Powers	Germany	ex	def	def	def	def	ex	nss	
	Italy	def	def	nss	def	ex	def	nss	
	Japan	nss	def	nss	def	def	def	nss	
								Axis total ➡	

ex = 'export' — this means that the country had enough for its own needs and was able to sell the rest abroad.

ss = 'self-sufficient' — this means that the country had enough for its own needs but did not have any left to sell abroad.

nss = 'not self-sufficient' — this means that the country did not have enough for its own needs.

def = 'deficient' — this means that the country did not have any supplies of this raw material.

 a) Use chart **A** to add up the raw material score for each of the countries at war. Score like this:

'export' = **5** points
'self-sufficient' = **3** points
'not self-sufficient' = **1** point
'deficient' = **0** points

So, for example, the USA gets **5** points for coal and **3** for iron towards its total. Write each total in the 'Total' column at the end.

b) Add up the totals for each of the two sides:

◆ USA, USSR and Britain;

◆ The Axis Powers – Germany, Italy and Japan.

What do these figures suggest about the chances the Axis Powers had of winning the war?

B How raw materials were used

Raw material	Uses
Coal	◆ used for explosives
Oil	◆ tank, truck, ship and aircraft fuel
Iron ore	◆ needed for manufacture of steel – used in tanks, ships, aircraft, shells, weapons, etc.
Copper	◆ electric wires and cables
	◆ cartridges and shells
Bauxite	◆ electric cables
	◆ moving parts in engines
Potash	◆ fertiliser for crops
Wheat	◆ bread

2 Now write a paragraph of 12–15 lines explaining **how** and **why** each of the seven types of raw materials listed in chart **B** was vital for a country at war.

3 Is it possible to identify **one** of these raw materials as being the most important, or are they all equally important? Give reasons for your answer.

7c *The triumph of the Axis: 1939–42*

By the middle of 1942 it seemed that the Axis Powers in Europe (Germany, Italy, and their allies) had almost won the war.

Britain was isolated and in danger of being invaded. In the Soviet Union, it seemed that Leningrad, Moscow and Stalingrad would soon be captured by the Germans as they advanced quickly eastwards.

In North Africa the German–Italian army advanced towards the vital Suez Canal. This was the lowest point for the Allies. Towards the end of 1942, Allied victories at Stalingrad and El Alamein turned events against the Axis Powers.

> Look at the map on the second sheet and use it to answer the questions below.

1▷ Use either a colour or shading to highlight all the countries still **neutral** (not on either side) in 1942: Sweden, Turkey, Eire, Spain, Portugal, and Switzerland.

2▷ Use a different colour or shade for the Axis Powers and their allies: Germany, Italy, Hungary, Romania, Slovakia, Finland, and Bulgaria.

3▷ Colour or shade Britain and the USSR: the two Allied Powers in Europe.

4▷ Colour or shade all the territory conquered by the Axis Powers between 1939 and 1942:

Poland (September 1939);
Norway, Belgium, Holland (all May 1940);
France (June 1940);
Estonia, Latvia, Lithuania (all July 1941);
Yugoslavia (1941);
Greece (1941);
Area A (1941–42);
Area B (1942).

5▷ For each of the occupied areas listed in Question 4 there is a box on the map. In this box write the date in which the area was occupied or surrendered. Use the information given in Question 4.

6▷ Using the information on the map, write a few sentences to explain why the Axis Powers were so sure that they had won the war by the middle of 1942.

7c *(continued)*

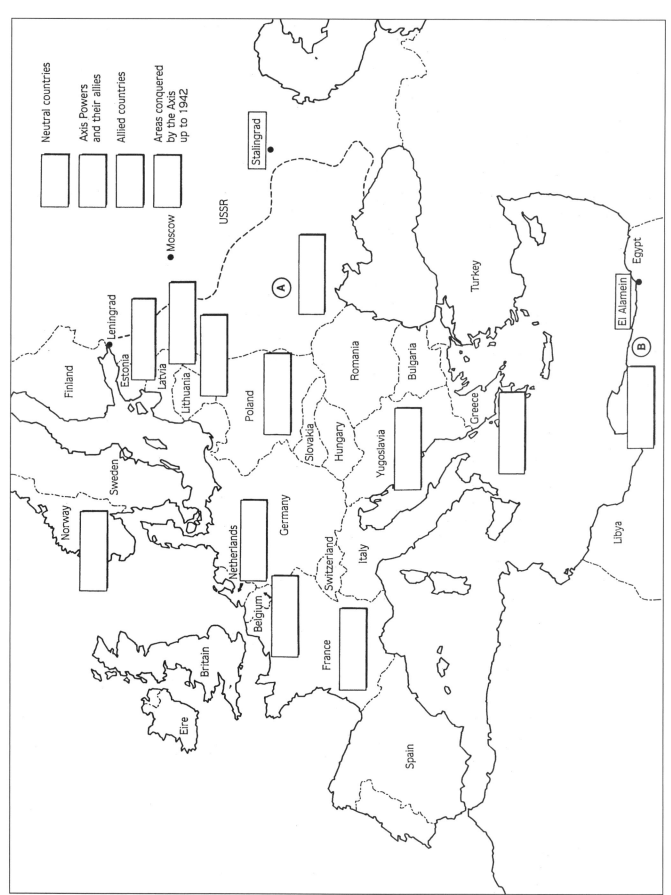

Neutral countries

Axis Powers and their allies

Allied countries

Areas conquered by the Axis up to 1942

Stalingrad

USSR

Moscow

A

Leningrad

Estonia

Latvia

Lithuania

Poland

Finland

Sweden

Norway

Netherlands

Belgium

Britain

Eire

France

Germany

Switzerland

Italy

Slovakia

Hungary

Yugoslavia

Romania

Bulgaria

Greece

Turkey

Egypt

El Alamein

B

Libya

Spain

7D D-Day dilemmas: *The invasion problem*

The problems involved in the invasion of German-occupied France by British, American and Canadian troops were huge. The Germans had plenty of time to prepare for the attack.

The best place for an invasion by sea was the French port of Calais, because:

✦ the harbour was big and deep enough to allow ships to dock and unload supplies;

✦ it was the point nearest to England.

However, it was also the most heavily defended part of the French coast because that's where the Germans expected the attack.

General Eisenhower, the American commander of the Allied forces, decided that the Allies must attack where it was not expected. This would give an element of surprise. He chose Normandy. But there were problems:

✦ Normandy was much further away than Calais;

✦ The water around the coast was too shallow for supply ships to get close enough to unload.

The plan could only work if some form of artificial harbour could be built. The answer was 'Mulberry'.

The solution ➡ | MULBERRY

Before Mulberry could be constructed, troops and tanks had to be landed on the beach to attack the German defences. Flat-bottomed landing craft were used for this. If the attack was successful and the beach made safe, then Mulberry could be built.

Mulberry was built by towing huge hollow concrete blocks – codenamed 'Phoenix' – across the Channel and then sinking them just off the shore on the French coast. These acted as a breakwater and kept the sea inside the harbour calm so that supplies could be unloaded. Supply ships, carrying ammunition, fuel, food and heavy equipment, docked beside flexible steel roadways. These roadways were lifted off the ships by cranes, and were strong enough to carry trucks and tanks.

Now move on to the two Activities on the separate sheets. First, complete the table in Activity 1, about where the invasion of France should take place. Then do Activity 2, about how the Mulberry harbour worked.

7D *(continued)*

You have been asked by Eisenhower to draw up a report on whether to launch the invasion of France at Calais or Normandy. Eisenhower has told you that there are four points to think about. These are in the first column of the table below. You have to comment on how suitable Calais and Normandy are in each case. Two boxes have already been filled in as examples.

Complete the table, and then write your decision at the bottom, with your reasons.

Where should the landing be: Calais or Normandy?

	Calais	Normandy
Closeness to England		
Element of surprise	The Germans are expecting an attack here and so there would be no element of surprise.	
Suitability of unloading supplies		The water is too shallow to allow ships to get close enough to unload supplies. However, our secret artificial harbour, Mulberry, has solved this problem.
Strength of German Defence		

Conclusion

I recommend that the invasion takes place at _____ because:

_____

_____

_____

_____

Activity 2

Look at this illustration of the Mulberry harbour used for the Normandy landings. There are five boxes to describe how the harbour worked. Fill in each of these boxes. You will find the necessary information on the first page of this worksheet.

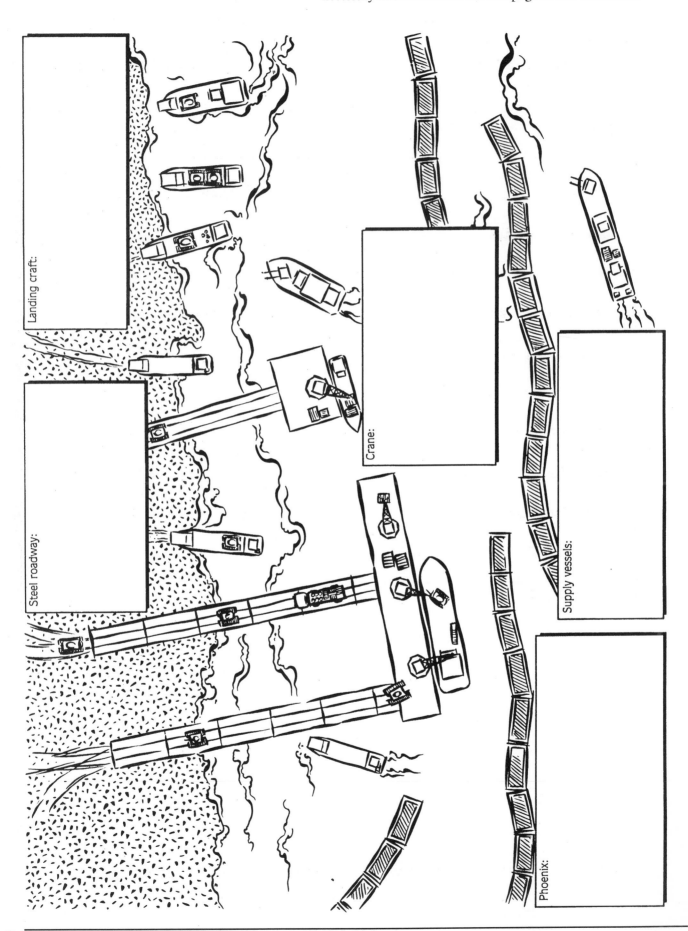

Landing craft:

Steel roadway:

Crane:

Supply vessels:

Phoenix:

7E Heads and tails

Pair up each of the entries in Column **A** with the correct one in Column **B** and then explain the link between them.

For example, 'The Rhineland' in Column **A** goes with '1936' in Column **B** because it was in 1936 that Hitler's troops invaded the Rhineland.

You will find the answers in Chapter 7 of your textbook (you will need to look at the sources carefully). After each item in Column **A** is the page number where you will find the answer.

Column A	Column B
Stalingrad (page 55)	June 1941
Hirohito (page 49)	British tank production in 1944
Manchuria (page 49)	7 December 1941
Abyssinia (page 49)	German aircraft production in 1939
Sudentenland (page 50)	Daladier
The Rhineland (page 51)	March 1938
Austria (page 51)	1931
French Prime Minister (page 51)	1935
8295 (page 52)	Emperor of Japan
Caucasus (page 55)	Czechoslovakia
18m tonnes (page 54)	Oil
Pearl Harbor (page 55)	Russian steel production in 1941
Midway (page 55)	Pacific turning-point
5000 (page 56)	Russian turning-point
Operation Barbarossa (page 53)	1936

7F *Understanding the text*

The answers to these questions are in Chapter 7 of your textbook. They are about the major events of the Second World War. At the end of each question is a page number where you should look for the answer.

1 ▷ What happened when German armed forces invaded Poland in September 1939? (page 51)

2 ▷ What was the main purpose of the League of Nations? (page 50)

3 ▷ Who lived in the Sudetenland region of Czechoslovakia? (page 50)

4 ▷ What country did Hitler occupy in March 1938? (page 51)

5 ▷ Who were the three major Axis Powers? (page 53)

6 ▷ What was the codename for the German invasion of Russia? (page 53)

7 ▷ Against which country did Japan launch a surprise attack in December 1941? (page 55)

8 ▷ What did the battle of El Alamein stop the German–Italian army from capturing? (page 55)

9 ▷ What did the Russian victory at Stalingrad stop the Germans from capturing? (page 55)

10 ▷ Where in France did the British and US forces land on June 6, 1944? (page 56)

Summary activity

Use the two paragraphs below as a summary of what you have read in Chapter 7. Complete the sentences and give your paragraphs the title 'The Second World War'.

If you get stuck, choose the missing word from the list at the bottom of the page, but try using Chapter 7 on its own first.

'The aim of the League of Nations was to keep the _____ and stop wars. Britain and _____ were its most important members. But they were not willing to stand up to _____ Germany and its dictator, Adolf Hitler. Eventually, Hitler went too far. When he invaded _____ in September 1939, both Britain and France declared war on Germany. At first, the Axis Powers – Germany, Italy and _____ – won many victories. But from _____ onwards, the Allies – the USA, Britain and Russia – turned the war round with victories at Midway, El Alamein and _____ .

The Axis Powers lost the war in 1945 because they did not have enough vital raw materials like _____ . Without this, their planes could not fly, their ships sail or their trucks move. The United States produced huge numbers of planes and _____ and eventually Germany and Japan were forced to surrender in _____ .'

Choose from: **1942   1945   peace   tanks   Nazi   oil**

Poland   Stalingrad   France   Japan

Attitudes towards the enemy in the Second World War

What did ordinary British and American soldiers feel about their German enemies in the Second World War? One of the good things about studying the Second World War is that there are still many people alive who fought in it, and so historians can still ask them.

You will need to read Sources E, F and G (pages 66–67) of Chapter 8 in your textbook before answering these questions.

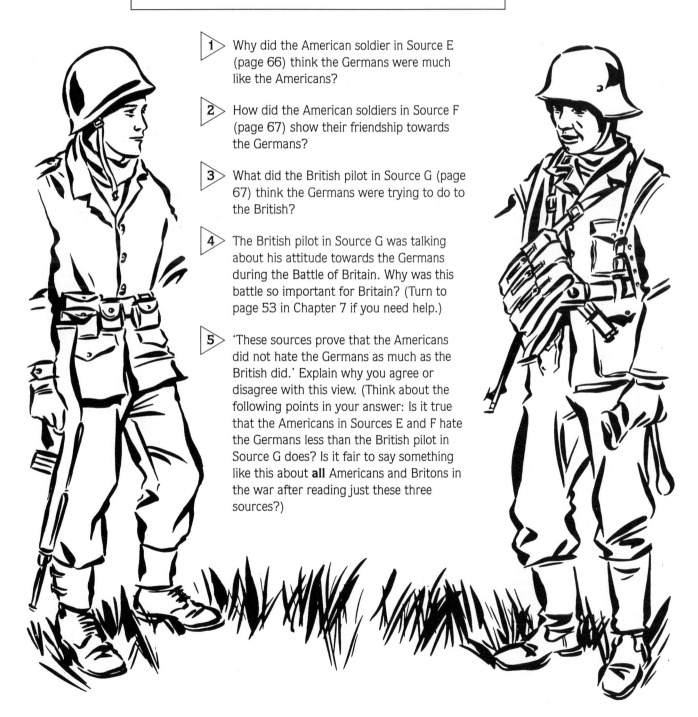

1 ▷ Why did the American soldier in Source E (page 66) think the Germans were much like the Americans?

2 ▷ How did the American soldiers in Source F (page 67) show their friendship towards the Germans?

3 ▷ What did the British pilot in Source G (page 67) think the Germans were trying to do to the British?

4 ▷ The British pilot in Source G was talking about his attitude towards the Germans during the Battle of Britain. Why was this battle so important for Britain? (Turn to page 53 in Chapter 7 if you need help.)

5 ▷ 'These sources prove that the Americans did not hate the Germans as much as the British did.' Explain why you agree or disagree with this view. (Think about the following points in your answer: Is it true that the Americans in Sources E and F hate the Germans less than the British pilot in Source G does? Is it fair to say something like this about **all** Americans and Britons in the war after reading just these three sources?)

Women and the First World War

Look at Sources **A** and **B** in Chapter 4 (page 27). Source **A** is a poster showing women waving goodbye to soldiers as they march off to war. When men went off to fight in the war, women were called on by the government to take their places in the factories and on the land. Women were encouraged to do all sorts of jobs they had never done before, like the one in Source **B**. It shows some women working in a munitions factory during the war.

1▷ Source **A** suggests that mothers and wives wanted their sons or husbands to fight in the war. How does the poster make this clear?

2▷ How would this poster encourage more men to volunteer to fight in the war?

3▷ Source **B** shows women working in a munitions factory. Before the war, a job like this would have been considered unsuitable for women. Why?

4▷ Why did many women change their minds during the war about the kind of jobs they could do? (Clue: You'll find one answer in the first paragraph of this sheet; see if you can think of others to do with patriotism and pay.)

10A The Cold War

Below are a list of ten pairs. For each of the pairs write a sentence
to explain how they are linked.

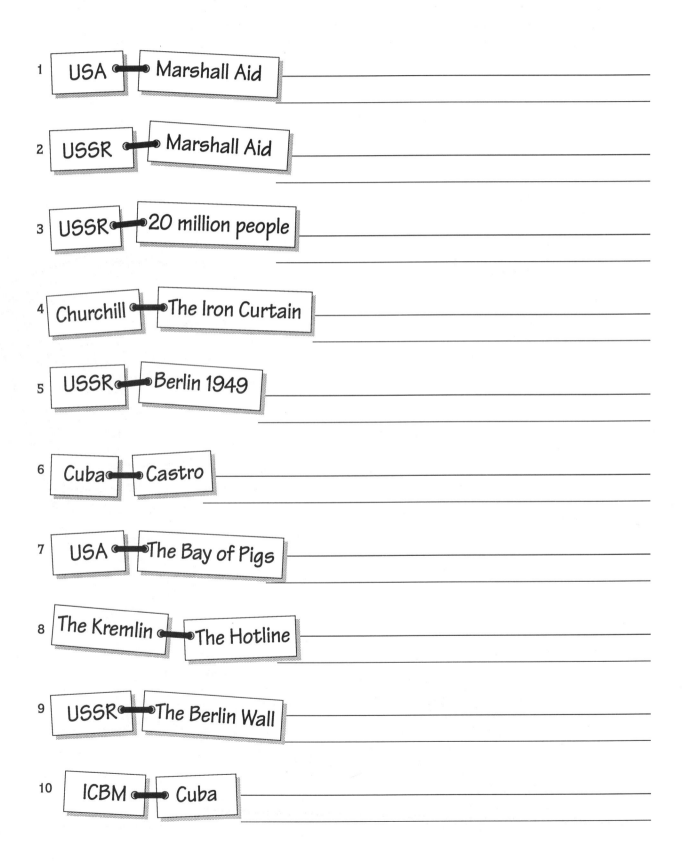

1 USA — Marshall Aid

2 USSR — Marshall Aid

3 USSR — 20 million people

4 Churchill — The Iron Curtain

5 USSR — Berlin 1949

6 Cuba — Castro

7 USA — The Bay of Pigs

8 The Kremlin — The Hotline

9 USSR — The Berlin Wall

10 ICBM — Cuba

 10B Cuba

American U2 spy planes have been flying over Cuba and they have taken photographs of the island. These photographs show that the Russians are building nuclear missile sites on Cuba. If the Russians are allowed to finish building these sites they will be able to target their missiles at some of the biggest US cities. The Russians do not seem to have brought any missiles to Cuba yet, but photographs from other U2 planes show that ships carrying the missiles are on their way from Russia.

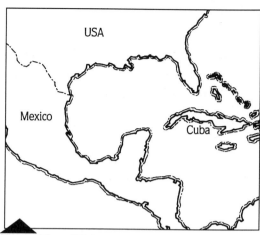

The position of Cuba

> **Your task is to help President Kennedy decide what to do next.**
>
> The table below shows five different courses of action which you could advise the President to take. Each policy has advantages and disadvantages. Some of these have already been filled in. You must fill in the rest. Then you must decide which of the five courses of action you believe that President Kennedy should follow. You can choose as many as you like.

Options	Advantages	Disadvantages
1 Quarantine Cuba. This means stopping and searching all ships heading for Cuba.	The Russians will not be able to attack the USA if the missiles cannot get to Cuba.	The Russians may well decide that stopping their ships is an act of war and so they may launch a nuclear attack on the USA
2 Prepare for nuclear war with Russia.		
3 Increase flights of U2 spy planes over Cuba.	This will tell you if any missiles have arrived. It will also show if there are more bases.	
4 Invade Cuba and capture the missile sites.		If you fail, the Russians will be able to claim that Cuba needs the missiles to defend itself from US attacks.
5 Order CIA to assassinate Castro.		

I will advise President Kennedy to follow option(s) _____

10c Cuba

Photographs taken by U2 spy planes show that the Russians are building nuclear missile sites on Cuba. There do not appear to be any missiles on the island yet. However, U2 planes have photographed Russian ships on their way to Cuba and these show missiles being carried on their decks. President Kennedy has asked your advice on what to do next.

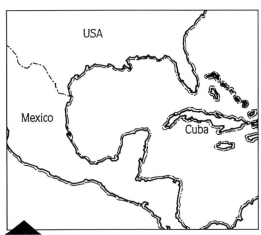

The position of Cuba

> Complete the table below. Five courses of action are available. Each one involves the risk of nuclear war with Russia. Decide what are the advantages and disadvantages of each option. When you have completed the table, decide which option you will be advising President Kennedy to use. You can choose more than one option.

Options	Advantages	Disadvantages
1 Quarantine Cuba. This means stopping and searching all ships heading for Cuba.		
2 Prepare for nuclear war with Russia.		
3 Increase flights of U2 spy planes over Cuba.		
4 Invade Cuba and capture the missile sites.		
5 Order CIA to assassinate Castro.		

I advise President Kennedy to follow option(s) _____

I am advising the President to follow this option/these options because: _____

_____

If you have chosen more than one option, place them in order of importance _____

Why have you chosen this order? _____

_____

10D *The nuclear threat*

In the years following World War Two, a number of things happened which made it possible for a nuclear war to break out. In 1962 the world really did believe that a nuclear war was going to happen, as a result of the Cuban Missile Crisis.

The Timeline on the right gives the dates of the major events which increased the danger of a nuclear war.

Fill in the name of these events in the correct boxes, next to the date when they happened (1962 has already been completed).

You will find the answers in Chapter 10, on pages 82 and 83 of your textbook.

Nuclear Threat Timeline

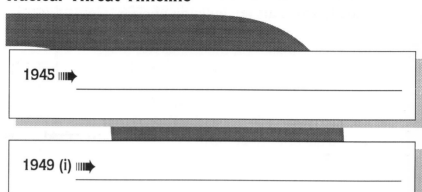

1945 ⇒ _____

1949 (i) ⇒ _____

(ii) ⇒ _____

1954 ⇒ _____

1955 ⇒ _____

1957 ⇒ _____

1958 ⇒ _____

1962 ⇒ _____*Cuban Missile Crisis*_____

The United Nations crossword

Fill in the answers on the grid. You will find the answers in the unit
'The United Nations' on pages 85–87 of your textbook.

Clues

1 The UN agency which helped refugees made homeless by the Second World War. (5 letters)

2 The UN charter was signed here on 25 June 1945. (2 words – 3 letters, 9 letters)

3 The General in charge of the UN troops in Korea. (9 letters)

4 A disease wiped out by 1980. (8 letters)

5 One of the permanent members of the Security Council. (5 letters)

6 There was a civil war in this country in 1994. (6 letters)

7 This country provided 50 per cent of the UN land forces during the Korean War. (3 letters)

8 The agency in charge of improving the health of the people of the world. (3 letters)

9 A vote to stop the UN taking action. (4 letters)

Korea

Map 1

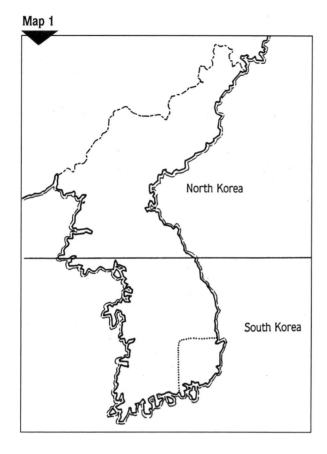

Map 2

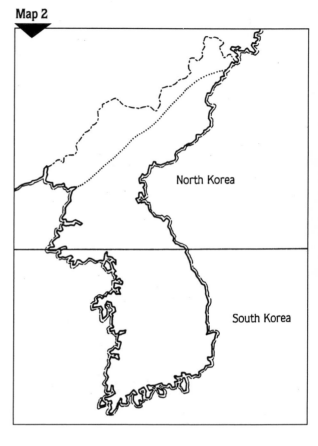

Map 3

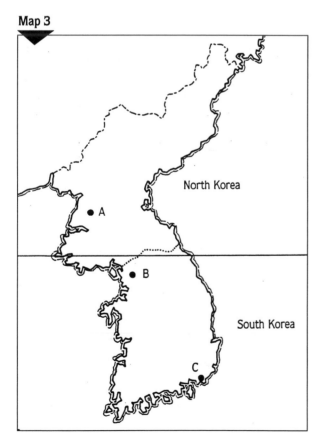

1 ▷ For each of the 3 outline maps of Korea, colour the area controlled by the **UN forces** in one colour and the area controlled by the **Communists** in another colour.

2 ▷ What has occurred to change the situation in **Map 1** to that shown in **Map 2**?

3 ▷ What is the name given to the border between the North and South of Korea in **Map 3**?

4 ▷ Name cities A, B and C on **Map 3**.

10G Korea

Map 1

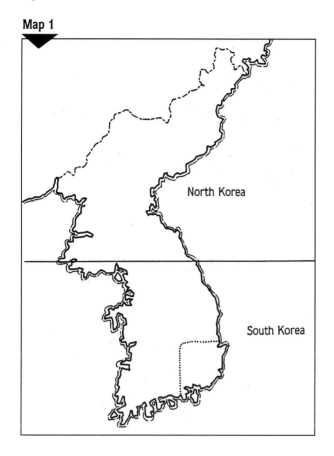

North Korea

South Korea

Map 2

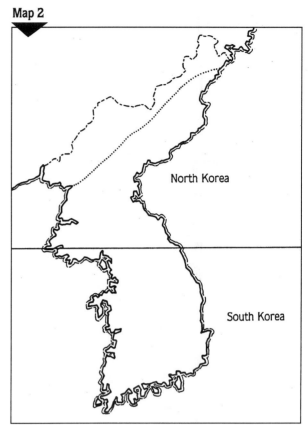

North Korea

South Korea

Map 3

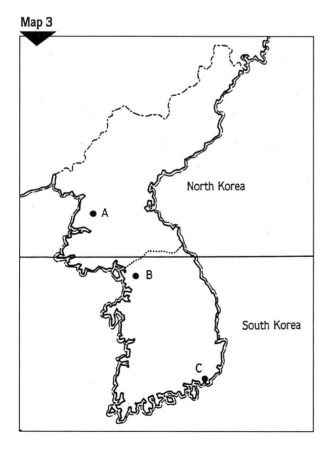

North Korea

● A

● B

South Korea

C
●

1 ▷ For each of the 3 outline maps of Korea, colour the areas controlled by the **UN forces** in one colour and those controlled by the **Communists** in another colour.

2 ▷ Explain what has led to the change in the area controlled by each side in Maps **2** and **3**.

3 ▷ Name the cities A, B and C on **Map 3**.

4 ▷ Was there a winner in the Korean War? Use Chapter 10 on pages 85 and 86 of your textbook to help you answer this. You will need to consider the following points in order to decide.

a) Did the North control more territory at the end of the war?

b) Did the Americans stop the spread of Communism?

c) Did the UN show it could control countries who used war to gain territory?

The end of Empire

A Map of Africa showing three former British colonies

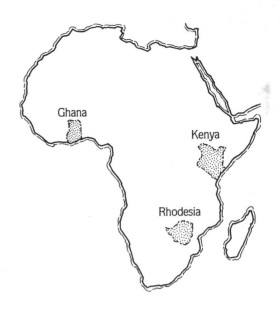

Ghana
Kenya
Rhodesia

B Dates of independence from Britain

Ghana	Kenya	Rhodesia (became Zimbabwe)
1957	1963	1980

In 1964 the white colonists of Rhodesia had declared UDI (Unofficial Declaration of Independence), that is they left British control without Britain's permission. This was to prevent Britain declaring Rhodesia independent and ruled by the native Black majority population.

C Ghanaian independence according to a British geographer

The income per person of its 7.5 million population is not far short of £90 a year and though this is not very high by European standards it is three times as high as...some other African states. This is one reason why Ghana was able to achieve independence before her neighbours. Linked with this greater prosperity was an older and more developed educational system which had by the 1950s produced a potential administrative élite [ruling class].'

D

Rhodesian population in 1964

White	217,000
Black	3,970,000
Others (mainly Asians)	20,000
Total	**4,207,000**

E The relationship of Whites and Blacks in Rhodesia, according to a British geographer

State expenditure on whites is twenty times as high for whites as for Africans. Both in jobs and in education the Europeans still form a privileged caste [class]. The privileges can only be maintained by the continuance of White political control.'

F

Exports in 1964

Ghana	£ 115.6 million
Kenya	£ 47 million
Rhodesia	£ 126.5 million

Sources all quoted in The Geography of African Affairs by Fordham (Penguin, 1968)

1 What reasons are given in **C** to explain why Ghana was one of the first African countries to be granted independence from Britain?

2 Why do the think the author mentions education as an important reason?

3 Does **F** agree with **C** about to the main reason why a country would be granted independence?

4 Look at **C**, **D** and **E**.

a) What percentage of Rhodesia's population was Black in 1964?

b) In what ways are the positions of the native Black people different in the two countries of Rhodesia and Ghana?

c) Why do you think the White people of Rhodesia had spent so little money on the education of Black people?

d) None of these sources mention the size of the White population in Ghana. Do you think that there were as many Whites in Ghana as in Rhodesia? Give at least two reasons for your answer.

e) Ghana became independent from Britain in 1957. It was another 23 years before this happened to Rhodesia. What evidence can you find in these sources to help explain this fact?